English as She is Spoke

English as She is Spoke

by Jose de Fonseca & Pedro Carolino

Start Publishing LLC.
Visit our website at http://start-publishing.com/

Printed in the United States of America

Print ISBN: 978-1-63596-119-5

Table of Contents:

Introduction

FROM the time of Shakspere downwards, wits and authors innumerable have made themselves and the public more or less merry at the expense of the earlier efforts of the student of a strange tongue; but it has been reserved to our own time for a *soi disant* instructor to perpetrate—at his own expense—the monstrous joke of publishing a Guide to Conversation in a language of which it is only too evident that every word is utterly strange to him. The Teutonic sage who evolved the ideal portrait of an elephant from his "inner consciousness" was a commonplace, matter-of fact person compared with the daring visionary who conjures up a complete system of language from the same fertile but untrustworthy source. The piquancy of Senhor Pedro Carolino's *New Guide of the Conversation in Portuguese and English* is enhanced by the evident *bona fides* and careful compilation of "the little book," or as Pedro himself gravely expresses it, "for the care what we wrote him, and for her typographical correction."

In short, the *New Guide of the Conversation in Portuguese and English* was written with serious intent, and for the purpose of initiating Portuguese students into the mysteries of the English language. The earlier portions of the book are divided into three columns, the first giving the Portuguese; the second what, in the opinion of the author, is the English equivalent; and the third the English equivalent phonetically spelt, so that the tyro may at the same time master our barbarous phraseology and the pronunciation thereof. In the second part of the work the learner is supposed to have sufficiently mastered the pronunciation of the English language, to be left to his own devices.

A little consideration of the shaping of our author's English phrases leads to the conclusion that the materials used have been a Portuguese-French phrase-book and a French-English dictionary. With these slight impedimenta has the daring Lusitanian ventured upon the unknown deep of a strange language, and the result, to quote again from the Preface, "May be worth the acceptation of the studious persons, and especially of the Youth, at which we dedicate him particularly," but will at all events contribute not a little to the Youth's hilarity.

To begin with the vocabulary; it is perhaps hardly fair to expect a professor of languages to trouble himself with "Degrees of Kindred," still, such titles as "Gossip mistress, a relation, an relation, a guardian, an guardian, the quatergrandfather, the quater-grandmother," require some slight elucidation, and passing over the catalogue of articles of dress which are denominated "Objects of Man" and "Woman Objects," one may take exception to "crumbs" and "groceries," which are inserted among plates and cruets as ordinary table garniture.

Among what are denominated "Eatings" we find "some wigs," "a dainty dishes," "a mutton shoulder," "a little mine," "hog-fat," and "an amelet": the *menu* is scarcely appetising, especially when among "Fishes and Shellfishes" our Portuguese Lucullus sets down the "hedgehog," "snail," and "wolf." After this such trifles as "starch" arranged under the heading of "Metals and Minerals," and "brick" and "whitelead" under that of "Common Stones" fall almost flat; but one would like to be initiated into the mysteries of "gleek," "carousal," and "keel," which are gravely asserted to be "Games." Among "Chivalry Orders" one has a glimmering of what is intended by "Saint Michaelmas" and "Very-Merit"; but under the heading of "Degrees," although by a slight exercise of the imagination we can picture to ourselves "a quater master," "a general to galeries," or even a "vessel captain," we are entirely nonplussed by "a harbinger" and "a parapet."

Passing on to "Familiar Phrases," most of which appear to be old friends with new faces, Senhor Carolino's literal cribs from the French become more and more apparent, in spite of his boast in the Preface of being "clean of gallicisms and despoiled phrases." "Apply you at the study during that you are young" is doubtless an excellent precept, and as he remarks further on "How do you can it to deny"; but study may be misdirected, and in the moral, no less than in the material world, it is useful to know. "That are the dishes whom you must be and to abstain"; while the meaning of "This girl have a beauty edge" is scarcely clear unless it relates to the preternatural acuteness of the fair sex in these days of board schools and woman's rights.

Further on the conversationalist appears to get into rough company, and we find him remarking "He laughs at my nose, he jest by me," gallicé "*Il me rit au nez, il se moque de moi*"; "He has me take out my hairs," "He does me some kicks," "He has scratch the face with hers nails," all doubtless painfully translated with the assistance of a French-English dictionary from "*Il m'a arraché les cheveux*," "*Il me donne des coups-de-pied*," "*Il m'a lacere la figure de ses ongles.*" It is noticeable that our instructor as a rule endeavours to make the possessive pronoun agree with the substantive in number and gender in orthodox Portuguese fashion, and that like a true grammatical patriot he insists upon the substantive having the same gender as in his native tongue; therefore "*às unhas*" must be rendered "hers nails" and "*vóssas civilidádes*" "yours civilities." By this time no one will be disposed to contradict our inimitable Pedro when he remarks "*E factéo*" giving the translation as "He has the word for to laugh," a construction bearing a suspicious resemblance to "*Il a le mot pour rire.*" "He do the devil at four" has no reference to an artful scheme for circumventing the Archfiend at a stated hour, but is merely a simulacrum of the well-known gallic idiomatic expression "*Il fait le diable à quatre.*" Truly this is excellent fooling; *Punch* in his wildest humour, backed by the whole colony of Leicester Square, could not produce funnier English. "He burns one's self the brains," "He was fighted in duel," "They fight one's selfs together," "He do want to fall," would be more intelligible if less picturesque in their original form of "*Il se brûle la cervelle,*" "*Il s'cet battu en duel,*" "*lis se battent ensemble,*" "*Il manque de tomber.*" The comic vein running through the "Familiar Phrases" is so inexhaustible that space forbids further quotation from this portion of the book, which may be appropriately closed with "Help to a little most the better yours terms," a mysterious adjuration, which a reference to the original Portuguese leads one to suppose may be a daring guess at "*Choisissez un pen mieux vos paroles.*"

In the second part, entitled "Familiar Dialogues," the fun grows fast and furious. Let us accompany our mad wag upon "The walk." "You hear the bird's gurgling?" he enquires, and then rapturously exclaims "Which pleasure! which charm! The field has by me a thousand charms"; after this, to the question "Are you hunter? Will you go to the hunting in one day this week?" he responds "Willingly; I have not a most pleasure in the world. There is some game on they cantons." Proceeding from "game" to "gaming" we soon run aground upon the word "*jeu,*" which as we know does duty in French both for a game and a pack of cards. "At what pack will you that we does play?" "To the cards." Of course this is "*A quel Jeu voulez vous que nous Jouions?*" "*Aux cartes;*" and further on "This time I have a great deal pack," "*Cette fois j'ai un jeu excellent!*"

Now let us listen to our friend at his tailor's: his greeting is perky—almost slangy. "Can you do me a coat?" he enquires, but quickly drivels down to "What cloth will you do to?" and then to the question "What will you to double (*doubler*) the coat?" obtains the satisfactory answer "From something of duration. I believe to you that." After requesting to have his garment "The rather that be possible," he overwhelms the procrastinating man of cloth with the stern remark "You have me done to expect too," evidently a bold version of "*Vous m' avez fait trop attendre,*" which draws forth the natural excuse "I did can't to come rather." Passing by a number of good things which one would like to analyse if space permitted, we arrive at "For to ride a horse," a fine little bit of word painting almost Carlylean in its grotesqueness. "Here is a horse who have a bad looks. He not sail know to march, he is pursy, he is foundered. Don't you are ashamed to give me a jade as like? he is unshoed, he is with nails up; it want to lead to the farrier." "Let us prick (*piquons*) go us more fast, never I was seen a so much bad beast; she will not nor to bring forward neither put back." "Strek him the bridle," cries the horsedealer, "Hold him the rein sharters." "Pique stron gly, make to marsh him." "I have pricked him enough. But I can't to make marsh him," replies the indignant client. "Go down, I shall make marsh," declares the dealer; upon which the incensed equestrian rejoins "Take care that he not give you a foot kicks," and the "coper" sardonically but somewhat incoherently concludes with "Then he kicks for that I look? Sook here if I knew to tame hix."

After the "Familiar Dialogues" we come upon a series of letters from celebrated personages, who would be puzzled to recognize themselves in their new dresses; and a collection of anecdotes which may be taken singly after dinner as a gentle promoter of digestion; the whole being appropriately concluded with "Idiotisms and Proverbs," between which it must be confessed the distinction is purely imaginary; the following are a few gems: "Its are some blu stories" (*contes bleus*); "Nothing some money, nothing some Swiss," "He sin in trouble water" (confusion of *pécher* and *pêcher*). "A horse baared don't look him the tooth," "The stone as roll not heap up not foam," *mousse* meaning both foam and moss, of course the wrong meaning is essential to a good "idiotism." "To force to forge, becomes smith" (*a force de forger on devient forgeron*). "To craunch the marmoset" and "To fatten the foot" may terminate the list, and are incontestably more idiotic, although scarcely so idiomatic as "*Croquer le marmot*" and "*Graisser lapatte.*"

The column in Portuguese which runs throughout the original work is omitted, and only a sufficient number of the English extracts are culled to enable the reader to form a just idea of the unintentionally humorous style that an author may fall into who attempts to follow the intricacies of "English as she is spoke" by the aid of a French dictionary and a phrasebook.

It is to be trusted the eccentric "Guide" to which this short sketch is intended to serve as Introduction—and, so far as may be, elucidation—is not a fair specimen of Portuguese or Brazilian educational literature; if such be the case the schoolmaster is indeed "abroad," and one may justly fear that his instruction—to quote once more the Preface—"only will be for to accustom the Portuguese pupils, or foreign, to speak very bad any of the mentioned idioms."

Author's Preface.

A CHOICE of familiar dialogues, *clean of gallicisms, and despoiled phrases, it was missing yet to studious Portuguese and brazilian Youth; and also to persons of others nations, that wish to know the Portuguese language. We sought all we may do, to correct that want, composing and divising the present little work in two parts. The first includes a greatest vocabulary proper names by alphabetical order; and the second forty three* Dialogues *adapted to the usual precisions of the life. For that reason we did put, with a scrupulous exactness, a great variety own expressions to english and Portuguese idioms; without to attach us selves (as make some others) almost at a literal translation; translation what only will be for to accustom the Portuguese pupils, or-foreign, to speak very bad any of the mentioned idioms.*

We were increasing this second edition with a phraseology, in the first part, and some familiar letters, anecdotes, idiotisms, proverbs, and to second a coin's index.

The Works *which we were confering for this labour, fond use us for nothing; but those what were publishing to Portugal, or out, they were almost all composed for some foreign, or for some national little acquainted in the spirit of both languages. It was resulting from that carelessness to rest these* Works *fill of imperfections, and anomalies of style; in spite of the infinite typographical faults which some times, invert the sense of the periods. It increase not to contain any of those* Works *the figured pronunciation of the english words, nor the prosodical accent in the Portuguese; indispensable object whom wish to speak the english and Portuguese languages correctly.*

We expect then, who the little book (for the care what we wrote him, and for her typographical correction) that may be worth the acceptation of the studious persons, and especially of the Youth, at which we dedicate him particularly.

Translations

Defects of the body.

A blind	A left handed
A lame	An ugly
A bald	A squint-eyed
A deaf	

Degrees of kindred.

The gossip	the quater-grandfather
The gossip mistress	The quater-grandmother
The Nurse	A guardian
A relation	An guardian
An relation	A widower
An widow.	

Trades.

Starch-maker	Porter
Barber	Chinaman
Coffeeman	Founder
Porkshop-keeper	Grave-digger
Cartwright	Tradesman
Tinker, a brasier	Stockingmender
Nailer	Lochsmith

Objects of man.

The boots	The lining
The buckles	The clogs
The buttons-holes	The wig
The buskins	the morning-gown, night-gown

Woman objects.

The busk	The paint or disguise
The sash	The spindle
The conet	The patches
The pumps	The skate

Servants.

Coochmann	Spendth
Running footman	Business-man

Groome.

Diseases.

The apoplexy	The megrime
The scrofulas	The whitlow
The melancholy	The rheumatisme

The vomitory.

Parties a Town.

The butchery	The low eating house
The cause-way	The obelis-ks
The sink	The prison, geol

Kitchen utensils.

The skimming-dish	The spark
The potlid	The fire
The pothanger	The smoke
The spunge	The clout

The jack.

Of the bed.

The bed wood	The feet's bed
The bed battom	The pillar's bed

The head's bed.

For the table.

| Some knifes | Some groceries |

Some crumb.

Eatings.

Some sugar-plum	Hog fat
Some wigs	Some marchpanes
A chitterling sausages.	An amelet
A dainty-dishes	A slice, steak
A mutton shoulder	Vegetables boiled to a pap

Seasonings.

Some wing	Some pinions
Some cinnamon	Some hog'slard
Some oranges	Some verjuice

Drinkings.

| Some orgeat | Some paltry wine |

Some sirup or sirop

Quadruped's beasts.

Lamb	Roebuck
Ass	Dragon
Shi ass	wild sow
Ass-colt	Lioness

Ram, aries | Dormouse

Birds.

Becafico | Heuth-cock
Calander | Whoop
Stor | Pea cock
Yeung turkey | Pinch
          Red-Breast, a robin

Insects-reptiles.

Asp, aspic | Fly
Morpion | Butter fly
          Serpent.

Fishes and shell-fishes.

Calamary | Large lobster
Dorado | Snail
A sorte of fish | Wolf
Hedge hog | Torpedo
          Sea-calf.

Trees.

Lote-tree lotos | Service-tree
Chest nut-tree | Jujube-tree
          Linden-tree.

Flowers.

Anemony | Mil-foils
Blue-bottle | Hink
          Turnsol.

Hunting.

Hunting dog	Picker
Relay dog	Gun-powder
Hound dog	Priming-powder
Hound's fee	Hunts man

Colours.

White	Gridelin
Cray	Musk

Red.

Metals and minerals.

Starch	Latten
Cooper	Plaster

Vitriole

Common stones.

Loadstones	White lead
Brick	Gum-stone

Weights.

Counterpoise	An obole
A pound an half	A quater ounce.

Games.

Football-ball	Pile
Bar	Mall
Gleek	Even or non even
Carousal	Keel

Perfumes.

Benzion	Pomatum

| Perfume paw | Storax |

On the church.

| The sides of the nef | The little cellal |
| The holywater-pot | The boby of the church |

Solemn-feasts.

| The Deads-day | The Vigil |
| The Twelfth-Dat | The Visitation |

Ecclesiastical dignities.

Incumbent	General of an order
Canon	Penitentiary
Canoness	Theologist
Chanter, a clerk	General curate

Chivalry orders.

Black eagle	Elephant
Avis, advice	Honour Legion
Calatrava	Saint Michaelmas
Very-merit.	

Degrees.

A cannoneer	A general to galeries
A vessel captain	A great admiral
A harbinger	A king a lieutenant
A parapet	A quater master
A army general	A vice admiral's ship

Military objects.

| The bait. | The fire pan |
| An arquebuse | A bomb ketch |

A bandoleer | The military case
A fusil, a gun.

Music's instruments.

A flagelet | A dreum
A hurdy-gurdy.

Chastisements.

A fine | To break upon
Honourable fine | To tear off the flesh
To draw to four horses

Familiar Phrases.

Go to send for.
Have you say that?
Have you understand that he says?
At what purpose have say so?
Put your confidence at my.
At what o'clock dine him?
Apply you at the study during that you are young.
Dress your hairs.
Sing an area.
These apricots and these peaches make me and to come water in mouth.
How do you can it to deny?
Wax my shoes.
That is that I have think.
That are the dishes whose you must be and to abstain.
This meat ist not too over do.
This ink is white.
This room is filled of bugs.
This girl have a beauty edge.
It is a noise which to cleave the head.
This wood is fill of thief's.
Tell me, it can one to know?
Give me some good milk newly get out.
To morrow hi shall be entirely (her master) or unoccupied.
She do not that to talk and to cackle.
Dry this wine.
He laughs at my nose, he jest by me.
He has spit in my coat.
He has me take out my hairs.
He does me some kicks.
He has scratch the face with hers nails.
He burns one's self the brains.
He is valuable his weight's gold.
He has the word for to laugh.
He do the devil at four.
He make to weep the room.
He was fighted in duel.

They fight one's selfs together.
He do want to fall.
It must never to laugh of the unhappies.
He was wanting to be killed.
I am confused all yours civilities.
I am catched cold.
I not make what to coughand spit.
Never I have feeld a such heat
Till say-us?
Till hither.
I have put my stockings outward.
I have croped the candle.
I have mind to vomit.
I will not to sleep on street.
I am catched cold in the brain.
I am pinking me with a pin.
I dead myself in envy to see her.
I take a broth all morning.
I shall not tell you than two woods.
Have you understanded?
Let him have know?
Have you understand they?
Do you know they?
Do you know they to?
The storm is go over.
The sun begins to dissipe it.
Witch prefer you?
The paving stone is sliphery.
The thunderbolt is falling down.
The rose-trees begins to button.
The ears are too length.
The hands itch at him.
Have you forgeted me?
Lay him hir apron.
Help-to a little most the better yours terms.
Dont you are awaken yet?
That should must me to cost my life.
We are in the canicule.
No budge you there.
Do not might one's understand to speak.

Where are their stockings, their shoes, her shirt and her petlicot?

One's can to believe you?

One's find-modest the young men rarely.

If can't to please at every one's.

Take that boy and whip him to much.

Take attention to cut you self.

Take care to dirt you self.

Dress my horse.

Since you not go out, I shall go out nor I neither.

That may dead if I lie you.

What is it who want you?

Why you no helps me to?

Upon my live.

All trees have very deal bear.

A throat's ill.

You shall catch cold one's.

You make grins.

Will some mutton?

Will you fat or slight?

Will you this?

Will you a bon?

You not make who to babble.

You not make that to prate all day's work.

You interompt me.

You mistake you self heavily.

You come too rare.

Familiar Dialogues

For to wish the good morning.

How does your father do?
He is very well.
I am very delight of it. Were is it?
I shall come back soon, I was no came that to know how you are.

For make a visit in the morning.

Is your master at home?
Yes, sir.
Is it up.
No, sir, he sleep yet.
I go make that he get up.
It come in one's? How is it, you are in bed yet?
Yesterday at evening, I was to bed so late that
I may not rising me soon that morning.
Well! what you have done after the supper?
We have sung, danced, laugh and played.
What game?
To the picket.
Whom I am sorry do not have know it!
Who have prevailed upon?
I had gained ten lewis.
Till at what o'clock its had play one?
Un till two o'clock after mid night.
At what o'clock are you go to bed.
Half pass three.
I am no astonished if you get up so late.
What o'clock is it?
What o'clock you think is it?
I think is not yet eight o'clock.
How is that, eight 'clock! it is ten 'clock struck.
It must then what I rise me quickly.
Adieu, my deer, I leave you. If can to see you at six clock to the
  hotel from , we swill dine togetter.

Willingly. Good by.

For to dress him self.

John, make haste, lighted the fire and dress-me.
Give me my shirt.
There is it sir.
Is it no hot, it is too cold yet.
If you like, I will hot it.
No, no, bring me my silk stocking's.
Its are make holes.
Make its a point, or make to mend them.
Comb me, take another comb. Give me my handkarchief.
There is a clean, sir.
What coat dress you to day?
Those that I had yesterday.
The tailor do owe to bring soon that of cloth.
Have you wexed my shoes? I go wex its now.
It must that I may wash my hands, the mouth and my face.

The walk.

Will you and take a walk with me?
Wait for that the warm be out.
Go through that meadow.
Who the country is beautiful! who the trees are thick!
Take the bloom's perfume.
It seems me that the corn does push alredy.
You hear the bird's gurgling?
Which pleasure! which charm!
The field has by me a thousand charms.
Are you hunter? will you go to the hunting in one day this week?
Willingly; I have not a most pleasure in the world. There is some
  game on they cantons?
We have done a great walk.

The weather.

We shall have a fine weather to day.

There is some foggy.
I fear of the thunderbolt.
The sun rise on.
The sun lie down.
It is light moon's.

For to write.

It is to day courier day's; I have a letter to write.
At which does you write?
Is not that? look one is that.
This letter is arrears.
It shall stay to the post. This pen are good for notting. During I
   finish that letter, do me the goodness to seal this packet; it is
   by my cousin.
How is the day of month?
The two, the three, the four, etc.
That is some letter to me.
Go to bear they letter to the post.

The gaming.

Do you like the gaming?
At what pack will you that we does play?
To the cards.
Waiter, give us a card's game.
What is the trump?
The club's king.
Play, if you please.
The heart's aces.
We do ought.
This time I have a great deal pack.

With the tailor.

Can you do me a coat?
What cloth will you do to?
From a stuff what be of season.

How much wants the ells for coat, waist coat, and breeches?
Six ells.
What will you to double the coat?
From some thing of duration. I believe to you that
When do you bring me my coat?
The rather that be possible.
Bring you my coat?
Yes, sir, there is it.
You have me done to expect too.
I did can't to come rather.
It don't are finished?
The lining war not sewd.
It is so that do one's now.
Button me.
It pinches me too much upon stomack.
The sleeves have not them great deal wideness?
No, sir, they are well.

With a hair dresser.

Your razors, are them well?
Yes, Sir.
Comb-me quickly; don't put me so much pomatum. What news tell me?
  all hairs dresser are newsmonger.
Sir, I have no heared any thing.

For to breakfast.

John bring us some thing for to breakfast.
Yes, Sir; there is some sousages. Will you than I bring the ham?
Yes, bring-him, we will cup a steak put a nappe clothe upon
  this table.
I you do not eat?
How you like the tea.
It is excellent.
Still a not her cup.

For to ask some news.

It is true what is told of master M?

Then what is told of him?
I have heard that he is hurt mortally.
I shall be sowow of it, because he is a honestman.
Which have wounden him?
Do know it why?
The noise run that is by to have given a box on the ear
  to a of them.

For to buy.

I won't have a good and fine cloth to make a coat.
How much do you sell it the ell?
We thout overcharge you from a halfpenny, it cost twenty franks.
  Sir, I am not accustomed to cheapen: tell me the last price.
I have told you, sir, it is valuable in that.
It is too much dear, I give at it, eighteen franks.
You shall not have what you have wished.
You did beg me my last word, I told you them.
Well, well, cut them two ells.
Don't you will not more?
No, at present.

For to dine.

Go to dine, the dinner is ready.
Cut some bread; here is it, I don't know that boiled meat is good.
Gentilman, will you have some beans?
Peter, uncork a Porto wine bottle.
Sir, what will you to?
Some pears, and apples, what wilt you?
Taste us rather that liquor, it is good for the stomach.
I am too much obliged to you, is done.

For to speak french.

How is the french? Are you too learned now?
I could to tell some word's that I know by heart.
Not apprehend you, the french language is not difficult.
I know it, and she have great deal of agreeableness. Who I would
  be. If I was know it! It must to study for to learn it. How long

there is it what you learn it? It is not yet a month. How is
called your master?

It is called N

I know him it is long; he has teached a many of my friends. Don't
he tell you that it must to speak french?

For to see the town.

Anthony, go to accompany they gentilsmen, do they see the town.

We won't to see all that is it remarquable here.

Admire this master piece gothic architecture's.

The chasing of all they figures is astonishing indeed.

The streets are very layed out by line and too paved.

There is it also hospitals here?

It not fail them. What are then the edifices the worthest to
have seen?

It is the arsnehal, the spectacle's hall, the cusiom-house and
the Purse.

We are going too see the others monuments such that the public
pawnbroker's office, the plants garden's the money office's,
the library.

To inform oneself of a person.

How is that gentilman who you did speak by and by.

Is a German.

Tongh he is German, he speak so much well italyan, french, Spanish,
and english, that among the Italyans, they believe him Italyan,
he speak the frenche as the Frenches himselves. The Spanishesmen
belie ve him Spanishing, and the Englishes, Englisman.

It is difficult to enjoy well so much several langages.

For to ride a horse.

Here is a horse who have a bad looks. Give me another; I will
not that. He not sail know to march, he is pursy, he is foundered.
Don't you are ashamed to give me a jade as like? he is undshoed,
he is with nails up; it want to lead to the farrier.

Your pistols are its loads?

No; I forgot to buy gun-powder and balls. Let us prick. Go us more fast never I was seen a so much bad beast; she will not nor to bring forward neither put back.

Strek him the bridle, hold him the reins sharters. Pique stron gly, make to marsh him.

I have pricked him enough. But I can't to make march him.

Go down, I shall make march.

Take care that he not give you a foot kick's.

Then he kicks for that I look? Sook here if I knew to tame hix.

With a watch maker.

I bring you a watch that want to be ordered.

I had the misfortune to leave fall down the instant where I did mounted, it must to put again a glass.

I want not a pendulum? I have them here some very good.

Don't you live me her proof againts? I shall not accept that this condition.

For to visit a sick.

How have you passed the night?

Very bad. I have not sleeped; I have had the fever during all night. I fell some pain every where body.

Live me see your tongue. Have you pain to the heart?

Are you altered?

Yes, I have thursty often.

Your stat have nothing from lrouble some.

What I may to eat?

You can take a broth.

Can I to get up my self?

Yes, during a hour or two.

Let me have another thing to do?

Take care to hold you warme ly, and in two or three days you shall be cured.

For to travel.

Where you go so?

I am going to Cadiz.

Have you already arrested a coach?

Yes, sir, and very cheap.

There is it some danger on the highway?

It is not spoken that.

They speak not that may have some robbers on the woods?

It have nothing to fear, or in day neither the night.

Don't we does pass for a?

No, sir, they leave it to left.

Let us take patience, still some o'clock, and we shall be in the
end of our voyage.

With a inn keeper.

What you give us for to take supper.

Gentlemen, what you will have.

Give us a pigeon couple, a piece of ham and a salad.

What have us expended?

Theaccout mount in little the supper, the bed and the breakfast,
shall get up at thirty franks.

From the house-keeping.

I don't know more what I won't with they servants.

I tell the same, it is not more some good servants. Any one take
care to sweep neither to make fire at what I may be up.

How the times are changed! Anciently I had some servants who were
divine my thought. The duty was done at the instant, all things
were cleanly hold one may look on the furnitures now as you do
see. It is too different, whole is covered from dust; the
pierglasses side-boards, the pantries, the chests of drawers, the
walls selves, are changed of colours. I do like-it too much.

Believe me, send again whole the people; I take upon my self to
find you some good servants for to succeed them.

Ah! what I shall be oblige to you of it!

For the comedy.

Were you go to the theatre yesterday?

Yes, sir; I won't to see the new play in which did owed to play
and actress which has not appeared on any theatre.

How you think her?

She has very much grace in the deeds great deal of exactness on
the declamation, a constitution very agreable, and a delightful
voice.
What you say of the comedy? Have her succeded? It was a drama;
it was whistted to the third scene of the last act.
Because that?
It whant the vehicle, and the intrigue it was bad conducted.
So that they won't waited even the upshot?
No, it was divined.
In the mean time them did diliver justice to the players which
generaly have play very well.
At the exception by a one's self, who had land very much hir's
part.
It want to have not any indulgence towards the bat buffoons.
Have you seen already the new tragedy? They
praise her very much.
It is multitude already.
Never I had seen the parlour so full.
This actor he make very well her part.
That piece is full of interest.
It have wondered the spectadors.
The curtains let down.
Go out us.

The hunting.

There is it some game in this wood?
Another time there was plenty some black beasts and thin game, but
the poachers have killed almost all.
Look a hare who run! let do him to pursue for the hounds! it go
one's self in the ploughed land.
Here that it rouse. Let aim it! let make fire him!
I have put down killed.
Me, I have failed it; my gun have miss fixe.
I see a hind.
Let leave to pass away, don't disturte it.
I have heard that it is plenty pardridges this year.
Have you killed also some thrushes.
Here certainly a very good hunting.

The fishing.

That pond it seems me many multiplied of fishes. Let us amuse
  rather to the fishing.
Here, there is a wand and some hooks.
Silence! there is a superb perch! Give me quick the rod. Ah!
  there is, it is a lamprey. You mistake you, it is a frog! dip
  again it in the water.

With a furniture tradesman.

It seems no me new.
Pardon me, it comes workman's hands.
Which hightness want you its?
I want almost four feet six thumbs wide's, over seven of long.

For embarking one's self.

Don't you fear the privateers!
I jest of them; my vessel is armed in man of war, I have a
  vigilant and courageous equipage, and the ammunitions don't want
  me its.
Never have you not done wreck?
That it is arrived me twice.

With a gardener.

Shall I eat some plums soon?
It is not the season yet; but here is some peaches what does ripen
  at the eye sight.
It delay me to eat some wal nuts-kernels; take care not leave to
  pass the season.
Be tranquil, I shall throw you any nuts during the shell is green
  yet.
The artichoks grow its?
I have a particular care of its, because I know you like the
  bottoms.
It must to cup the trees.
It should pull the bad grasses up.

The books and of the reading.

Do you like the reading good deal too many which seem me?
That is to me a amusement.

The field.

All the fields that you see thither were been neglected; it must I
    shall grub up and to plough its.
The ground seems me a little scour with sand and yet it may one
    make it bring up; I want be fumed time by time.

The writing.

Your pens have any notches, and its spit.
How do you like its? will you its are fine or broad?
I won't me also a wafer or some sealing wax and a seal.
In this drawer, there is all that, falding stick, rule, scraper,
    saud, etc.
There is the postman I go to put it him again.

With a bookseller.

What is there in new's litterature?
Little or almost nothing, it not appears any thing of note.
And yet one imprint many deal.
But why, you and another book seller, you does not to imprint some
    good wooks?
There is a reason for that, it is that you cannot to sell its. The
    actual-liking of the public is depraved they does not read who
    for to amuse one's self ant but to instruct one's.
But the letter's men who cultivate the arts and the sciences they
    can't to pass without the books.
A little learneds are happies enough for to may to satisfy their
    fancies on the literature.
Have you found the Buff on who I had call for?
I have only been able to procure the octodecimo edition, which is
    embellished with plates beautifully coloured.

With a dentist.

I have the teetht-ache.

Is it a fluxion, or have you a bad tooth?

I think that is a bad tooth; please you to examine my mouth?

You have a bad tooth; will you pull out this tooth?

I can't to decide me it, that make me many great deal pain.

Your tooth is absolutely roted; if you leave it; shall spoil the others.

In such case draw it.

I shall you neat also your mouth, and you could care entertain it clean, for to preserve the mamel of the teeth; I could give you a opiate for to strengthen the gums.

I thank you; I prefer the only means, which is to rinse the mouth with some water, or a little brandy.

With a laundress.

Who lhat be too washed, too many soaped, and the shirts put through the buck. You may be sure; never I do else.

For to swim.

I row upon the belly on the back and between two waters.

I am not so dexte rous that you.

Nothing is more easy than to swim; it do not what don't to be afraid of.

The french language.

Do you study?

Yes, sir, I attempts to translate of french by portuguese.

Do you know already the principal grammars rules?

I am appleed my self at to learn its by heart.

Do speak french alwais?

Some times: though I flay it yet.

You jest, you does express you self very well.

Familiar Letters.

Racine to M. Fitart.

My uncle what will to treat her beshop in a great sumptuouness, he
was go Avignon for to buy what one not should find there, and he had
leave me the charge to provide all things. I have excellent business,
as you see, and I know some thing more than to eat my soup, since I
know do to prepare it. I did learn that it must give to the first, to
second, and to the third service, by dishes that want to join, and
yet some thing more; because we does pretend make a feast at four
services without to account the dessert. Good bye, my dear sir, etc.

Mothe to the duchess of the Maine.

My lady, I have a complaint to present you. So much happy that might
be one's self, one have not all theirs eases in this world. Your
letters are shortest. You have plaied wonderfully all sentiments;
less her prattle, etc.

Montesquieu to the abbot Nicolini.

Allow me, my dear abbot, who I remind me of your friendship. I
recommend you M. of the Condamine. I shall tell you nothing, else he
is a of my friends. Her great celebrity may tell you from others
things, and her presence will say you the remains. My dear abbot, I
will love you even the death.

Anecdotes.

Guttler, a very rich man too many avaricious, commonly he was travel at a horse, and single for to avoid all expenses. In the evening at to arrive at the inn did feign to be indispose, to the end that one bring him the supper. He did ordered to the stable knave to bring in their room some straw, for to put in their boots he made to warm her bed and was go lo sleep. When the servant was draw again, he come up again, and with the straw of their boots, and the candle Avhat was leave him he made a small fire where he was roast a herring what he did keep of her pocket. He was always the precaution one to provide him self of a small of bread and one bring up a water bottle, and thus with a little money.

A blind did hide five hundred crowns in a corner of their garden; but a neighbour, which was perceive it, did dig up and took its. The blind not finding more her money, was suspect that might be the robed, but one work for take again it? He was going find the neighbour, and told him that he came to get him a council; than he was a thousand crowns which the half was hided into a sure part and I don't know if want, if to put the remains to the same part. The neighbour was council him so and was hasten to carry back that sum, in the hope soon to draw out a thousand. But the blind having finded the money, was seized it, having called her neighbour, he told him: "Gossip, the blind saw clearer than this that may have two eyes."

A man one's was presented at a magistrate which had a considerable library. "What you make?" beg him the magistrate. "I do some books," he was answered. "But any of your books I did not seen its.—I believe it so, was answered the author; I mak nothing for Paris. From a of my works is imprinted, I send the edition for America; I don't compose what to colonies."

One eyed was laied against a man which had good eyes that he saw better than him. The party was accepted. "I had gain, over said the one eyed; why I see you two eyes, and you not look me who one."

A english lord was in their bed tormented, cruelly of the gout, when was announced him a pretended physician, which had a remedy sure against that illness. "That doctor came in coach or on foot?" was request the lord. "On foot," was answered him the servant. "Well, was replied the sick, go tell to the knave what go back one's self, because if he was the remedy, which he exalt him self, he should roll a coach at six horses, and I would be send for him my self and to offer him the half part of my lands for to be delivered of my sickness."

A duchess accused of magic being interrogated for a commissary extremely unhandsome, this was beg him selve one she had look the devil. "Yes, sir, I did see him, was answer the duchess, and he was like you as two water's drops."

A Lady, which was to dine, chid to her servant that she not had used butter enough. This girl, for to excuse him selve, was bing a little cat on the hand, and told that she came to take him in the crime, finishing to eat the two pounds from butter who remain. The Lady took immediately the cat, was put into the balances it had not weighted that one an half pound.

A countryman which came through to Paris upon the bridge to the change, not had perceived merchandises in several shops. The curiosity take him, he come near of a exchange desk:—"Sir, had he beg from a look simple, tell me what you sell." The loader though that he may to divert of the personage:—"I sell, was answered him asse's heads."—"Indeed, reply to him the country-man, you make of it a great sale, because it not remains more but one in your shop."

The commander Forbin of Janson, being at a repast with a celebrated Boileau, had undertaken to pun him upon her name:—"What name, told him, carry you thither? Boileau: I would wish better to call me Drink wine." The poet was answered him in the same tune:—"And you, sir, what name have you choice? Janson: I should prefer to be named John-Meal. The meal don't is valuable better than the furfur?"

A physician eighty years of age had enjoicd of a health unalterable. Theirs friends did him of it compliments every days: "Mister doctor, they said to him, you are admirable man. What you make then for to bear you as well?—I shall tell you it, gentlemen he was answered them, and I exhort you in same time at to follow my exemple. I live of the product of my ordering without take any remedy who I command to my sicks."

A countryman was confessed to the parson to have robbed a mutton at a farmer of her neighbourhood. "My friend, told him the confessor, it must to return, or you shall not have the absolution.—But repply the villager, I had eated him.—So much worse, told him the pastor; you vill be the devil sharing; because in the wide vale where me ought to appear we before God every one shall spoken against you, even the mutton. How! repply the countryman, the mutton will find in that part? I am very glad of that; then the restitution shall be easy, since I shall not have to tell to the farmer: "Neighbour take your mutton again."

Plato walking one's self a day to the field with some of their friends. They were to see him Diogenes who was in to water untill the chin. The superficies of the water was snowed, for the reserve of the hole that Diogenes was made. "Don't look it more told them Plato, and he shall get out soon."

A day came a man consult this philosopher for to know at o'clock it was owe to eat. If thou art rich, told him eat when you shall wish; if you are poor, when you may do.

At the middle of a night very dark, a blind was walk in the streets with a light on the hand and a full jar upon the back. Some one which ran do meet him, and surprised of that light: "Simple that you are, told him, what serve you this light? The night and the day are not them the same thing by you!—It is not for me, was answering the blind, that I bring this light, it is to the and that the giddie swhich seem to you do not come to run against me, and make to break my jar."

Made in the USA
Monee, IL
01 December 2021

83645143R00022